4 $\frac{48}{8\cdot 7}$
4

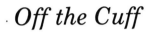

Off the Cuff

OFF
THE
CUFF

D. J. Trom

VANTAGE PRESS
New York / Washington / Atlanta
Los Angeles / Chicago

FIRST EDITION

Copyright © 1987 by D. J. Trom

Published by Vantage Press, Inc.
516 West 34th Street, New York, New York 10001

Manufactured in the United States of America
ISBN: 0-533-06955-6

Library of Congress Catalog Card No.: 86-90001

To my family,
a solid Rock of Gibraltar
to lean on in times of need

Off the Cuff

A

Abandon—Never give up anything, unless it is a bad habit.

Abbreviate—Some people should shorten their mouth span.

Abdicate—I don't think anybody should give up a crown, unless it gives him pain, but then Christ didn't give up his crown and it gave him pain.

Abduct—Never take anything that doesn't belong to you unless your leaving it with its owner is going to cause harm to somebody.

Abhor—To hate. Never hate anything or anybody unless it or he is dangerous to your health. Love is so much better.

Ability—Talents. Some people have few and some people have many. No matter how few or how many you have, be thankful.

Able—Having the power to do something. Some people can do many things at once. Some people can't chew gum and walk at the same time. Who cares? Just as long as you are satisfied with what you can do.

Abnormal—Different. Enjoy it. God made everything and everybody different.

Aboard—Come aboard Christ's ship. It will be well worth the journey.

Abolish—Don't end anything you will regret ending.

1

Abortion—A tough issue. Every case is different. Let God be the judge of which one was right or wrong.

Abound—Be plentiful with love and pass it on.

About-face—Don't be afraid to change your mind, especially if you were sinning.

Above—Where God is supposed to be, but he is everywhere.

Abrupt—Some people are this way. Don't let it get to you. The less you let people bother you, the better you will make it through life.

Absent without leave—Sometimes home is more important and awaits you.

Absolute—One hopes everyone is whole in body and soul; if you are not, do the best with what you have.

Absolution—A wonderful gift to be given, but don't repeat the sin; absolution may not be so easy the next time.

Absorb—Soak up all you can with your mind; it may not be as much as the next person can absorb, but at least it's something.

Abstinence—Refraining from liquor is fine, but a snort once in a while never hurt anybody. Just don't take too many snorts and drive.

Abstract—Not easy to understand. It breaks up the boredom of life once in a while.

Absurd—Some things are silly and ridiculous, but that makes the world go round.

Abundance—Share it with others that don't have as much.

Abuse—Report it if you see or suspect it. No person or animal should have to take it. Even the abuse of someone else's property is wrong and should be reported.

Accelerate—Increase the speed of the goodness in your heart toward the needs of others.

Accent—We may speak differently, but we are all after the same thing: to make it through the night.

Accept—Accept what you can. What you can't accept try to cope with the best you can.

Access—It would be wonderful if we could have the keys to some people's minds so they could be helped.

Accidental—Don't fret over things that you can't help.

Acclaim—Give praise to another person whenever the he deserves it—even a child who tries hard and still gets an F on a report card or finishes last in a race.

Accompany—Attend some event with somebody who is lonely.

Accommodate—Help whom you can, but leave some space for yourself.

Accomplish—Do what you can in one day, but don't tire yourself out. Tomorrow is another day.

Accord—I wish all countries would step in agreement with one another. What a safe world it would be for all God's children.

Account—Don't be afraid to take notice of your mistakes. We learn from them. Account for them and get on with your life.

Accumulate—If you pile up lots of material goods, share them with others who need them.

3

Ace—Make your hole in one to bring joy to others.

Ache—Don't let your aches control you. You must control your aches.

Achieve—Succeed with what you have to work with, but don't fault yourself for what you can't achieve because of lack of ability.

Acknowledge—Express thanks for the talents of others, for it is through recognition that we gain strength, not through envy.

Acne—I beat this; so can everyone else who gets it.

Acquaint—Get to know the nice things and people around you and be thankful for them.

Acquire—Get an education the best you know how and use it whenever possible.

Acre—Some people need a lot of land to spread their wings and some people a little. No matter how much land you have or how little, just be thankful you can spread your wings.

Acrobat—We are all walking on the tightrope of life. If you fall, just get back on again. It isn't how many times you fall that counts in life; it's that you get up each time.

Across—If you are having trouble getting to the other side, remember to take it slow, and you will make it.

Act—When you have the strength to help someone in need, do it. If you can't help, your prayers for them will provide the help they need.

Act of God—Something we don't understand but will when we meet the Master.

Active—Keep on moving. It is the only way you will see results of your goals in life.

Actor, Actress—A person who gets paid for doing what we do in real life for nothing.

Actual—Be sure what you tell is true. Lying can get to be a bad habit. Only lie when it is in the best interest of a person or thing.

Acute—I hope the only keeness and quickness you obtain are of the mind.

Ad lib—In situations that make your nervous, ad lib. It doesn't matter if something is not in the script.

Adam—Thank God he sinned. Life is too precious to be missed. Think of all the people you know.

Adapt—Don't let changes throw you. It is by changing we survive.

Addict—Be sure if you are hooked on something, it is a good thing, not drugs.

Address—Direct your energies to your problems, and they will be solvable.

Adequate—Make sure you have met your needs, then pass the leftovers to people who are in need of some.

Adhere—Stick to your ideas, even though you are the only one who believes in them. It is what you think of yourself as a person that counts, not what others think.

Adjust—When changes are needed to stay on the right track in life, make them. You can't go wrong when you use the judgment you were given naturally.

Administer—Help those in need. People in nursing homes who have nobody need your support. Maybe someday you will be helped in return.

Admiral—He should be kind to those who are under him. We are all born equal; he should remember that.

Admire—It is okay to have high regard for others, but save some for yourself.

Admit—Confess to your mistakes and take a different path, and you will find the true way to fulfill your life.

Admonish—Cautioning against someone's specific faults is okay, but never judge someone. Only God can do that.

Adopt—Fathering a child or giving birth to a child doesn't make a parent a parent. It is the love he or she shows toward a child that counts.

Adore—Adore God always.

Adorn—Don't put too many decorations on. Natural beauty is what counts.

Adrift—Don't let your mind steer too far from home base. It may be hard to get it back on the beaten path again.

Adult—What we are supposed to be when we are grown up, but it doesn't hurt to keep some of the child in you.

Adultery—Everybody thinks the other side is greener, but we forget that side has to be watered, too.

Advance—Move forward, but don't forget where you came from.

Advantage—No matter how many or how few benefits you have, use them to result in a good effect on others.

Advertise—Be sure that when you try and sell something, it is what you say it is. Don't let people down. Trust is built through salesmanship.

Advice—Don't give any out unless you have to. There is enough hot air floating around already.

Advocate—Make sure the support you give something will help others with their struggle through life.

Aerial—Let your ideas go high up in the air, then reach for them, and you will obtain them.

Affect—Be sure that no matter whomever or whatever you have influence on, your influence is good, and the results will benefit many people.

Affection—Don't hide love for others, it may be the thing that helps them make it through life.

Afflict—Never cause pain or suffering to someone unless in self-defense.

Affirm—Don't be afraid to stand up for your rights. It may be tough to speak out, but the words do come out of your mouth.

Affluent—If you have abundance, spread it around a little bit. You will be surprised at the good you can do.

Afford—If you can yield to someone else, go ahead, for there is more pleasure in giving than receiving.

Affront—Make sure if you encounter someone face to face, you are doing it for the right purpose and not for your selfish nature.

Afloat—If you find yourself free of trouble, grab somebody else to take along. Give them the joy of this sensation, too.

Afraid—Put your trust in the Lord, and you don't have to fear anything.

After—If you come later, don't feel bad. Take advantage of somebody else getting the path ready for you.

Afterlife—I believe there is one. I want to see the loved ones that have gone before me.

Afterthought—Better than no thought at all.

Again—Do something over and over until you get it right. Patience makes perfect.

Against—Better to be for something than against it.

Age—In God's world, it doesn't matter how old a person is and there is no such thing as age. God loves us all.

Agenda—Be sure your program includes being kind to humans, animals, Nature, and yourself.

Aggressive—Be bold and active when it comes to spreading good in the world. What a great world this would be if only more people would do this.

Agree—Try to be in accord with someone else, then march through life with this person. Two in step are sometimes better than one. Let that someone else be Christ.

Agriculture—Save it. It is the family farms that run America. Don't lose them. We can't afford to.

Aground—Don't let running aground stop you. There is only one way to go but up.

Ahead—Make sure that when you advance toward the future, your cause is acceptable to others, too.

Ail—Pray for recovery, then watch God's plan work for you.

Aim—Try to hit the right career for yourself, and you will go a long way. Don't give up if you miss. Try again.

Ain't—This word is in the dictionary, so don't be afraid to use it.

Air—God's gift to breathers. Help keep it clean.

Airplane—Soar as high as you can with your ideas. After you reach your goal, pave the way for a smooth landing.

Alarm clock—Don't curse it. Be thankful you can get of bed and go to work. Some people can't.

Alcohol—A little bit never hurt anybody. Just learn to control it. Don't drive drunk. Drink at home and you can flop into bed if you drink too much.

Alert—Watch out for Satan. Sin is his game. Don't play it. It may be hard not to, but the rewards will be great later on. Believe me.

Alibi—Don't make excuses for your mistakes. Take account of them and learn from them.

Allege—Don't assert anything without proof. It may be too hard to recall your mistake.

Allegiance—Be loyal to your true love.

9

Alleviate—Make less the pain of others whenever possible. Simon and Veronica helped Jesus on his way to the cross. So help others so their "crossful" paths won't be so painful.

Alliance—Form a union with others to work for a more peaceful world.

Allocate—Allot some time to your children every day. America's future depends on our children.

Allow—Don't forget about yourself when allotting time to others. Use some time to think about your life and your future.

Allowance—Teach your children the value of money. Give them an allowance, and tell them they have to budget it out for the week. Adult ways taught now will result in adult ways lived later.

All-purpose—Be useful in many ways. You never can tell when it will come in handy. In other words, be a jack of all trades, master of none.

Ally—Join with God and you will have a steady partner as you struggle through life.

Alone—You don't have to feel this, because he that is in you is stronger than what is outside the world.

Also-ran—There are no losers in a race. Everybody tries, so why care what position you wind up in?

Alternate—Always have one, two, or more choices ready to take action if at first you don't succeed in life.

Always—At all times remember your roots. They provide the foundation you can depend on for moral support.

Amateur—You don't have to earn money to do something to have fun. Just the pleasure of doing something should give you the joy for which you are looking.

Ambassador—Be God's representative in life. Help people find God and you will share their joy in this new discovery.

Ambition—Don't hide this. Bring it forth and go with the flow.

Ambush—Don't let Satan sidetrack you on the way to heaven.

America—God's gift to mankind.

Americans—They make America what it is today: great.

Amicable—A hello from a happy person can change the day for a depressed person. I know it did many times for me. So don't be afraid to give those hellos out; you never know whose life you're changing.

Amity—Let's pray for this every day. For when there are friendly and peaceful relations between nations, all God's children can enjoy peace.

Ammunition—You have the tool to get ahead in life: your brain. Use it. You'll be surprised at what comes forth.

Amnesty—I hope all governments learn to grant pardon to people who, in their hearts are working for a just cause.

Among—Surround yourself with good people, and maybe as a group you can change the world for the better.

Amount—See how much love you can spread through the world.

Amplify—Raise your voice for the needy and homeless. Your voice may be the only voice they have.

Amuse—If you are able to entertain people don't be afraid to do it. The joy you provide may be the only happiness they have in life.

Ancestor—It doesn't matter where you came from that counts. It is where you're going that matters.

Anchor—Don't let anything hold you down. Build up your strength and overcome it.

Angel—A good, steady companion to have around. I believe in guardian angels. Whether you believe they exist or not is beside the point. Why knock it if it is comforting to someone you know and love for him to believe he has a special helper for life?

Anger—It doesn't hurt to let off steam once in a while. Just be sure the fog isn't too thick for you to find your way back to your normal self.

Angry—Don't waste your time being angry. Your time would be better spent spreading happiness around the world.

Animals—Be kind to them. They conquer loneliness by their presence. Some people say when a certain person is bad, he or she acted just like an animal. That isn't so. The majority of animals don't act like some human beings do. So don't compare bad humans to animals.

Annoy—Don't bother anybody. Look in your mirror instead and pester that image until it produces the results you need to improve your life.

Annual—Recheck your life every year and see how you are coming along. Are you making progress toward a more productive life?

Anonymous—Nobody is unknown. God knows everybody.

Answer—The solution to your problems might be how hard you are praying in your requests. I think it takes your efforts and prayers to get the job done.

Anticipate—Take one day at a time. You will find life easier to cope with that way.

Antipathy—You may have a strong dislike for someone, but that isn't their problem; it's yours.

Antique—Any material thing that is really old is considered valuable. Why don't we treat people the same way? As they get older, we should seek out their wisdom instead of shutting them off from society.

Anxiety—Don't get uneasy about things. Everything comes out through the wash eventually.

Apart—When you are away from someone, you will realize how important he is in your life. So when you see him again, show your appreciation.

Apostle—I think we are all on a special mission for Christ. When you see a poor person, see Christ in him and help him. You then will have achieved the true purpose in life.

Apparel—If you have enough clothes, share with those that don't.

Appear—Look happy and it will spread to others.

Applause—Show praise when someone deserves it, especially your children.

Apple—They claim an apple keeps the doctor away. I don't believe it, because the doctors keep coming, or should I say we have to keep going to the doctor. Doctors don't make housecalls. Most of them don't, anyway.

Application—Use the skills given you and you will help make a happier world for all.

Appoint—Select yourself as a goodwill ambassador. Choose some deputies and spread your work around the world.

Appreciate—Think well of everything and it will be returned to you in a greater amount.

Apprentice—Learn your trade well and you will help America build its future.

Apron strings—It's not so bad to be tied to one's mother's or wife's apron strings. That's better than being tied to someone else's wife's or your mother-in-law's apron strings.

Arbor Day—Plant a tree and take care of it. Make America more beautiful, if that's possible.

Arctic—A beautiful region. It may be cold, but it shows God's creations in an unspoiled state. So don't complain about cold states or countries. Anybody who can survive winter in a cold region is a true human being at heart—the warmth of which you can't compare to anything.

Arithmetic—Make sure your pluses outweigh your minuses in life, and you will do all right.

Armful—Take as many people as you can in your arms and say "I love you" and hope they pass it on.

Armistice Day—Let's hope this is the last one.

Army—Bless them for they are defending our freedom.

Arnold—My father's name was Arnold. If all Arnolds were like him, we would have a more beautiful world.

Art—Enjoy it and support it. It is a joy to behold.

Artery—May your main road lead you to happiness.

Artificial—Be natural at all times. People will realize what they see in you is what you really are.

Ascend—Go up to your highest goal; then work at being better at it every day.

Ashamed—They are times you are going to feel humiliated or embarrassed, but don't let that overcome you.

Ask—Don't be afraid to seek information. If you learn enough someday, you will be the giver instead of the seeker.

Astray—If you think the right path is too beaten up, start a new one.

Astrology—It doesn't hurt to study the stars—just so you aren't so dazed by them that you forget to look where you are going on earth.

Atheists—They believe in something, because they believe in the idea of no God.

Athletes—I used to be jealous of athletes because of all the money they make, but not anymore. They work hard for it; they deserve it.

Atmosphere—Make the surrounding influence around you cheerful and people will enjoy you more.

Atomic bomb—You see one and that's one too many.

Audience—Don't be afraid of people. They provide an opportunity to have your ideas heard.

Audit—Take account of yourself once a year. See if there is room for improvement, then set up your goals for next year.

Auld lang syne—Remember the good old days and use your power to help recreate them.

Authority—Respect the power some people have. Someday it may be yours, too. Use it wisely and be kind to those below you.

Autograph—Give yourself a boost and buy yourself an autograph book and write your name in it everyday.

Automation—I don't mind progress as long as the robots are friendly and can strike up a good conversation.

Autumn—Proof there is a God. Look at all the beautiful colors!

Available—Avail yourself where charity is concerned.

"Ave Maria"—Sing it to someone you love.

Average—Nobody is average. God made a masterpiece out of everyone. Some didn't use their abilities the right way.

Avoid—Keep away from bad habits or else you may become a bad habit people will avoid.

Awake—Be sure you are this when you drive and that you aren't drunk.

Aware—Know your surroundings and you will know the direction you want to take in life's journey.

Away—Don't stay from home too long. The one keeping the home fires burning just may put them out.

Awe—Treat yourself once in a while and look in a mirror and discover the magic you possess.

B

Baby—A beautiful gift from God. Take care and love it, and you will see the wonderment grow before your eyes.

Baby-sitter—We never outgrow our need for one, especially if you are affected by mental illness.

Bach—Means music. I love him.

Bachelor—A male single. He can water the grass, but he doesn't have to cut it.

Backbone—No matter how weak or strong yours is, work with it.

Backward—It's okay to go toward the rear; just remember where the front is in case you ever change your mind.

Bacon—When you bring home the bacon, make sure it's fried right.

Bad—The opposite of good, but it can be corrected if you work at it.

Baggage—Don't be afraid to ask for help if the luggage in your life gets too heavy. Some people are better carriers than others.

Baldness—Having no hair is nothing to be ashamed of. A lot of people have hair but don't have the brains to go with it.

Balloon—I like them. They make everybody happy as they float in the air. They remind us of America: freedom.

Ballot—If you run for office and the only vote you get is the one you voted for yourself, that's not so bad. It shows you believe in yourself and in life. In order to make progress, you have to start with belief in self.

Banana—Eat plenty of them, because they are good for you.

Band—Let the music play on, just so it doesn't disturb the neighbors.

Bank—Make sure your spiritual account is banked up just as much as your monetary account.

Banner—Raise it once in a while and show where you stand.

Baptism—Everybody should experience this, because it gives you a fresh start in life.

Baptism of fire—Hell to go through, but how much stronger you are after it is over! My 1983 breakdown was a baptism of fire, but I survived.

Bar—It's better to walk home from one than to drive home. Plan to call a taxi if you are afraid to walk home or bring a friend along who will stay sober.

Barber—A good person to go to when you can't see where you're going anymore.

Bare—Some people shouldn't do this because it's hard on the eyes.

Bark—A good sound where burglars are concerned.

Barrel—A barrelful of laughs. Release some once in a while and make somebody happy.

Barrenness—Adopt a child and show your strength through the love you can provide.

Base—Build a strong foundation and you can launch anything.

Bastard—A name given a child born out of wedlock. But who cares about the circumstances of the child's birth. It is still a creation of God, to be loved and cared for. I will say, though, some men are bastards and it has nothing to do with the circumstances of their birth.

Bawl—If you hear this, help if you can or call for help if you can't help.

Be—Be good, be wonderful, and do whatever you must do to be natural.

Bead—A rosary a day keeps the Devil away.

Beam—Smile and you may start a habit that will be picked up by others.

Beauty—The inside kind is the more important because it isn't just skin deep. It has substance.

Bed—You have heard the saying "You made your bed; now lie in it." That's not so bad; just remember to straighten it out once in a while.

Beefcake—Don't feel bad if you don't have the body to be a Chippendale dancer. If you can get out of bed in the morning, what more could you ask for?

Beer—A good snort doesn't hurt anybody once in a while. The only thing is: Don't drive after too many snorts.

Begin—Start somewhere, like I did with this book. The first step is your most important one.

Behave—Treat others like you would want to be treated.

Believe—This will keep you going, because without it you don't have anything to hold onto.

Belong—Wherever you are, that is where you belong. Make it a better place for those who will remain after you are gone.

Bend—Bend the rules if it means survival for someone.

Berlin—May God give strength to those who live in this city.

Best—Sometimes the ones who finish last are the best. Maybe they did the best they could with the talent they had.

Beyond—Don't be afraid to go beyond the horizon. The rewards will be great if you are willing to take the chance.

Bible—Study it and live it. Read it even if you don't understand it. You won't walk alone through a storm if you have the knowledge of the Bible within you.

Bible Belt—This region tries to hold up the rest of the nation's pants.

Bicycle—Try to ride one every day. It is good exercise.

Bill—Don't overuse your charge accounts; otherwise, you will get too many bills. If you have trouble paying yours, see a financial advisor.

Bird—Don't you wish you could fly like one? Instead of driving away from troubles, you could fly.

Bisexual—Liking both sexes. I suppose it is better than liking one and hating the other, but maybe you should limit your sexual activity to members of the opposite sex.

Bitch—Believe it or not, there are some of these in the world.

Black—Opposite of white, but just as good.

Blame—When you are at fault, admit it, but don't let it hinder you.

Blessings—The people who make others happy when they are depressed.

Blind—They can see more, because when you are forced to use your imagination, you gain a type of sight you never knew you had.

Blockhead—Some people act this way and they shouldn't, because they have the means to do better.

Blond—I think blond people do have more fun. There are so many of them with smiles on their faces.

Blood bank—Thank God for those who donate.

Bloom—Bloom where you are planted. I stole this from the "Hour of Power" show, but it is true. From wherever you live, you can make a difference to the whole world if you do the best you can.

Blubber—Too much makes you overweight, so slim down and become part of a healthier you for the whole world to enjoy.

Boat—We are all in the same boat, but some row differently.

Body—Keep it in shape and if you ever have to strip you won't be so embarrassed.

Bomb—One going off is one too many.

Bone—Beauty is skin deep, so make sure your bones are healthy.

Book—Everyone should write one. Whether is gets published or not is beside the point. Once you get it out of your system, you feel good.

Boondocks—Don't be ashamed to admit you live in the hinterland. After all, that is where nature is the most beautiful.

Boring—If you are bored with life, go to a nursing home and do some volunteer work. When you go home, you will appreciate the difference.

Borrow—Be sure to return that which belongs to another, because a reputation built up of returning will insure future borrowing.

Boss—A person to be ignored when he gets under your skin or to listen to in order to decide what is trash and what is knowledge. Send the trash in one ear and out the other.

Boston rocker—Relax in one once in a while or in any other type of rocker, it does the heart good.

Bottle—Bottle up the good memories and let them out when you are feeling sad.

Bottom—From this position the only thing to do is ascend.

Bound—Be prepared to go home someday. It's a reward you will deserve if you live right.

Bout—Never give up the struggle. Strength is gained when you put up a fight.

Boutiques—I love them. I wish I had the guts to buy one.

Bowling—A fun game. Do it whenever you get a chance.

Boxing—I don't like boxing. I don't like to see people scarring each other.

Brace—Don't be ashamed to wear one. It is there to help you, not hinder you.

Braille—God bless him for inventing a system of writing for the blind.

Brain—Use whatever you got. It isn't the quantity that counts, but the quality.

Brake—When it comes to sin, do this.

Branch—Spread out and see how much you can learn.

Brand—It isn't the trademark that counts; it's the quality of performance.

Brave—Willing to face danger, pain, or trouble. You may not think you have this, but when the time comes, with God's help, you will find it.

Brawl—Avoid this and if you see one call the police.

Brazil—This country reminds me of coffee, which is a good picker-upper. I hope they keep it coming.

Break—Don't break anything that doesn't belong to you.

Breaking point—If you experience this, bounce back and start a mending point.

Bride—There must not be any homely women in the world, because everybody says the bride looks so pretty when they attend a wedding.

Bridesmaids—Remember the saying, "Always a bridesmaid, never a bride?" That's not so bad. A lot of the bridesmaids are cuter than the brides.

Briefcase—Just because you don't carry a briefcase to work doesn't mean your job isn't important. It's what you do with your hands, not what you carry, that counts.

Bright—Share your bright outlook on life with others, and maybe it will spread.

Bring—It doesn't matter who brings home the bacon, just so long as somebody brings it. If nobody can bring home the bacon in your home, don't be afraid to accept assistance. That's what it's there for.

Britain—I wouldn't want to live in this country, because the monarchy stays in the same family. At least in this country we get a change for sure every eight years.

Brotherhood—We all belong to the brotherhood of God. I wish everybody would act like it.

Bubble—If someone breaks yours, blow up another one.

Buck—Whether you pass the buck or stop the buck, be sure you save some of the buck. In your later years, it will come in handy to live on.

Buggy—I wish the buggies would come back, even though we would have to watch where we stepped. They didn't go as fast, but the beauty of the horses was worth the loss of time.

Build—Develop the strength inside of you, and then when you need it, reach down and use it with all the gusto you have.

Building—You can bomb a building, but you can't destroy the principles of the people that occupied that building.

Bullet—A bullet is powerless without a gun, and a gun is powerless without a hand. Let's learn to control all three.

Bum—What we save money for to become someday.

Buoyancy—Make a habit of it, and hope this habit is picked up by others.

Burnout—If this happens to you, don't let it bother you. Get your rest and then recharge yourself and go up the hill again.

Butterfly—Let this be a symbol of being free, not a symbol of an uneasy feeling in one's stomach. I have never seen a butterfly fly out of a person yet. Butterflies are beautiful; give them the credit due them.

BYOB—It's all right to go to a BYOB (Bring Your Own Bottle) party, but be sure you can BYOB (Bring Yourself On Back) when it comes time to go home.

Bypass—Don't be afraid to avoid something you fear. Practice your strength and the next time you won't bypass your fears.

C

Cabdrivers—Appreciate them; they have a dangerous job.

Cabin—A place to go and let your troubles float away on the lake or river or whatever.

Cactus—Put this under the seat of a slow riser.

Caddie—I think a golfer should carry his own clubs. With his strength built up by carrying the extra load, he could hit the ball farther.

Cadets—Cadets make me think of West Point, the place to be to learn how to be brave when it comes to defending freedom for the enjoyment of the rest of us, who are not such brave souls.

Café—In the wintertime when your rich friends are in a warm state and you are in a cold one, treat yourself to a cup of coffee and a doughnut in a café. A warm climate is wherever the heart desires it to be.

Calculate—Don't calculate your money before you have earned it.

Calendar—No matter what day or year it is, every second is different. So live for today, because yesterday is gone and tomorrow does not yet belong to you.

California—Where the movie stars are, but you can be one right where you are. Everybody's a star in the movie of their life.

Call—Call someone far away and let them know you care.

Calligraphy—Practice this, because once it is learned, you can make someone happy by writing letters in this style.

Calm—You have heard of the calm before the storm. What counts more is how calm you are after the storm.

Camel—Be like a camel: Store something in your heart and let it pour forth when the need is there.

Cameo—You may think your role in life is small but in God's eyes nobody can play your part in life better than you can.

Camera—Take a picture of someone you love, and if you lose them, remember the joy of them from the picture.

Campaign—If you campaign for a candidate and end on the short end of the stick, that's not so bad, because eventually it teaches you how to handle the long end of the stick when you get there.

Can—You can do anything you want to if you remember even in defeat you can overcome.

Cancer—Those who die from it pave the way for a cure of it.

Candid—Be honest at all times, because that will reveal you are a person to be trusted.

Candle—It is better to light a candle and share it with the whole world than to curse the darkness.

Cannon—If you really want to achieve your goal in life, go after it, making the sound of a cannon instead of that of a cap gun.

Canvas—Paint whatever your heart desires, no matter if nobody else understands it.

Cap—Wear one when your head is cold, no matter what anybody else thinks.

Capacity—If you have the ability to do something you'd better do it. It is when we use the resources from within that the resources outside become better.

Capital—Any town is capable of being a capital. The townspeople just have to work at the image they want to project.

Capital punishment—I think in some cases this is needed, because if you can't live according to the rules of society, you don't have the right to be part of society.

Captain—Learn to be a follower first; then you can be a captain.

Captive—You may be held prisoner, but no one can control how you will react to what he does to you.

Car—Why do they make cars that you can drive so fast? You can't drive that fast, because of the speed limits. I think some fools drive that fast whether they are allowed to or not.

Carbon copy—Why are there lawsuits when somebody copies someone else? You should have pride that somebody thought so much of your work he copied it.

Card—Send one to somebody who has nobody else.

Cardinal—There are more priests than cardinals, so don't feel bad if you aren't one. After all, it is the parish priest that is the hub of the church.

Care—Give it to those who need it.

Careful—As you walk through life, be careful not to step on something that will slow your pace.

Carousel—I like the merry-go-round. If you are a child at heart, ride it. You never outgrow your need for a ride on a carousel.

Carol—Cheer somebody up. Sing carols any time of the year.

Carpenter—A beautiful trade. They repair and build the wood products of the world, making it a better place for all of us to live.

Carrier pigeon—Bring them back. To preserve peace, send a message by pigeon.

Carrots—Rabbits don't wear glasses. Carrots must be good for something.

Carry—Besides carrying your own load, help somebody else if he needs it and if you have the strength to do it.

Cartoon—To relieve the pressures of life, watch a cartoon once in a while.

Cartwheel—If you feel overjoyed about something, do one in your front yard. Who cares what the neighbors think?

Case—When you go into court, be prepared. A case well prepared is a case well heard.

Castle—You may not live in one, but be thankful you have a roof over your head.

Castro—He should shave and he might not look so hateful.

Catastrophe—Handle it the best you know how, and with God's help you can start anew.

Catch—Catch a falling star and throw it back in the sky. Stars are meant to be shiners, not pocket-occupiers.

Catcher—I feel for this person. He has to bend his knees during the baseball game. He is between an opponent with a bat in his hands and a man with an inflated stomach. Also, a man who is suppose to be his friend is throwing a hard object at him.

Cause—If your cause is a just one, work hard for it, because efforts well spent will pay off in a more livable world for all.

Cave—Don't hide in one. Overcome your nervousness and be a part of life.

Cedar—Be sure your insulation for life is sturdy, because you are going to need it to survive the tough times.

Celebrate—Help a friend mark a special occasion, for having a friend is worth the effort put forth for the celebration.

Cemetery—Don't judge a person by the cemetery he is buried in, for some great people are buried in some shabby cemeteries.

Censor—Show concern for what your children are exposed to, because they are the world's future.

Center—If your life isn't the hub of the wheel, just remember: it is the spokes that hold the hub in place.

Certain—Be sure of your facts before you speak. There is enough hot air in the atmosphere already.

Challenge—The prospects for tomorrow depend upon how you accept the challenge of today.

Chance—To be a success, you have to take risks; otherwise, the enjoyment of succeeding won't be there.

Change—Change what you can and accept what you can't, with the exception being that you won't give up fighting for what you believe in.

Character—This is built by appreciating the talents of others and locating your own and being just as appreciative of them.

Chase—It is all right to chase a rainbow, but make sure once you catch it, you can handle it.

Cheap—You pay for what you get, so make sure your price is right.

Check—Bounce a basketball instead of a check.

Cheerful—If you are joyful, share it with the first sad person you see.

Cheesecake—I like the kind you eat, because there's more dressing on it.

Chestnut—Roast some any time of the year, and share some with a lonely person.

Chief—We need more Indians in order to control the chiefs.

Choices—Use common sense as much as possible, and you will make the right choices in life.

Choir—Sing in one; it is good exercise for your lungs. You don't need to sell a million records in order to sing. Everybody can sing; it just sounds different to different ears.

Christ—He died on the cross for everybody. He didn't care what color their skin was.

Christian—Somebody who believes in Christ, whether he goes to church every Sunday or not. Life is not easy, but Christ chose the path of thorns and survived, so why can't you?

Christmas—This happens every day, because every day the rebirth of Christ is happening in somebody's soul.

Christmas tree—Decorate it not with how much money can buy, but with things from the heart.

Church—You don't have to go to a building for worship. Faith is anywhere you seek your God and worship him.

Churchgoer—Some people who don't go to church act more Christian than some who attend regularly.

Circumstance—Don't try and understand your surroundings before you accept them, because with acceptance will come understanding.

City slicker—The opposite of a country hick; when a city slicker and a country hick get together, they have a slicking-hicking time.

Clap—When somebody makes you happier than you were before, they deserve your applause.

Clean—Keep the environment this way for the next generation to enjoy and for you to enjoy now.

Clergy—People who are close to God and want to share him with us.

Climax—When you reach the highest point, enjoy it, because the slide down is fast.

Climb—When you are not satisfied with ground level, do this.

Clock—Don't watch the clock, because when you are a prisoner of time, your time is without a stopwatch.

Cloud—Your life should be like a cloud. Float and pass on by your troubles.

Cloverleaf—A four-leaf clover is hard to find, because people obtain success from hard work, not luck.

Clown—A wonderful profession, because clowns make children and adults laugh.

Club—Form one and call it AHFE ("A Home for Everybody").

Coach—You can coach a team, but don't forget it is team play that wins games, not coach play.

Coffee break—Some people work through their break; others are on one all day. If everybody did their fair share of work, everybody would get a break and deserve it.

Coffin—Contains a dead body, but the spirit of the person goes on.

Cold—Good exercise for you, because you move fast in cold weather.

Cold-blooded—If you know somebody that is cold-blooded, thank God you're not. People remember the warmth you generate, not the chill.

Cold shoulder—Turn the other shoulder when somebody does this to you.

Collaborate—Do this at work with your fellow workers, and your bread and butter will seem more tasty.

Coma—People in a coma administer to the needs of others through their silence.

Comb—You can comb your hair all you want, but it's the hair that makes the hair, not the comb.

Comeback—Make this a good one, so you have a strong base built to stay in place.

Comment—Talk when it does somebody some good; otherwise, don't say anything. Idle chatter never helps anyone.

Commit—Pledge to help others and you will be helping yourself, too.

Common sense—More important than having a college degree.

Communism—Denial of freedom for some, so be the voice of those that don't have one.

Community—All the people living in a particular city, who are just as important as people living in a bigger city.

Companion—Be one to somebody that doesn't have one.

Compare—Don't compare anything; no two things are alike.

Compass—Know your directions and you will know your course in life.

Compassion—Don't be afraid to show it; some people need it to survive.

Compensate—Make up for the shortcomings of others, because if you make the world a better place to live, what does it matter where it comes from?

Compete—Enter the race and intend to win, but even coming in last is better than not being in the race at all.

Compromise—A settlement is the key to keeping things moving in a solid direction.

Concede—Acknowledge defeat, but don't accept it.

Conceit—Think it, but don't show it, because a positive attitude, not public display, shows results.

Concentrate—Focus on things that will make life better for you and others.

Concern—Somebody needs this every day, so give it where needed.

Concert—Go to one and thank God for the talents of others, because the results of long hours of practice went into your ears.

Conclude—Don't decide until the race is finished.

Condemn—Let God do this.

Confess—Be sorry for your sins, and be prepared to resist temptation when it comes your way again.

Confidence—You need this in order to avoid being flatter than a pancake.

Confidential—Avoid secrets. They tend to silence those people who could help.

Confine—Don't confine your mind, because a "think limit" makes for an unintelligent world.

Confusion—Don't get bewildered over things that will pass in time.

Congregation—People united in worship of God and working through his hands for the welfare of all.

Congress—Where no furnaces are needed in the wintertime because of all the hot air.

Connections—Make sure your connections in life move you forward toward the goals you laid out for yourself.

Conscience—Develop a good one and you will do all right in life.

Consequence—Be willing to pay the price when you step out of bounds, but after you have learned your lesson, pick up the pace you had before.

Conservation—Protect the natural resources, not just for future generations but for your generation to enjoy now.

Consider—Always observe the positives, never the negatives.

Console—Make someone less sad and tell them to pass it on.

Constant—Give faithful guidance to your children daily. Your efforts will pay off when your children are grown and shaping the world.

Constituent—Write your representative or president and give him the praise or hell he deserves, because it is through you he stays in office.

Constitution—Let's not be afraid to add amendments, because it is in freshness that we sustain principle.

Consumer—Be aware of the goods you buy and you will be a good consumer. Write to companies you think are cheating you and your fellow consumers.

Contrary—Don't be afraid to be different, because your difference may make the world a better place to live.

Control—Control your temper and your point will get across in a way more to your liking.

Convert—Be good to them; they came over to your side for a good reason.

Cook—Learn to do this and you can fend for yourself if need be. Also, if somebody is sick and can't feed himself, you can help him.

Cool—Some people think they are cool; don't let them freeze you out.

Cope—Learn to cope, because to make it through life, you have to deal with problems.

Cordial—Act this way toward people, and they will remember you for it.

Core—When you get to the center of the problem uproot the seeds and don't plant them again.

Cork—Don't let anybody get your cork, because a cork is hard to take back sometimes.

Corner—Don't sit in the corner; go to the center and be a part of the action.

Cornerstone—Make it a good one, you want it to last for a while.

Correct—Do it right the first time, and you won't have to do it over.

Correspondence—Take a correspondence course if you are too shy or nervous to go to school physically. Nothing must stop you from getting a college education if you desire one.

Cosign—Don't cosign something if you don't like responsibility.

Cosmetic—Some things look nice on the outside, but don't look inside, because you will be disappointed.

Costume jewelry—It may be imitation, but it glows just the same.

Cotton—If you had to pick it, you would appreciate it more.

Couch—Made to put your seat on, not to conceive on.

Council—Don't condemn a council from the sidelines; go to a council meeting and give your opinion.

Counsel—Give it if you understand the situation.

Count—Whether you are counting calories or sheep, don't count yourself out of anything until you take your last breath.

Counterfeit—People who work hard earn the real thing; they don't deal with artificial means.

Country—People left the country to move into towns, but the country never left them. Once you have felt the earth, nothing else feels the same.

Coupon—If products were sold cheaply enough, you wouldn't need coupons.

Courage—Everybody has courage. Some people have inside courage, which is felt but not seen.

Courtesy—Be courteous and you will be remembered for the sunshine you spread and not for the sadness some spread.

Cow—You think the world is dangerous now? Wait until cows start flying.

Coward—Don't judge a coward by his colors, because colors change and so can people.

Cowbell—Ring one when cows start flying, and maybe they will come down.

Cowboy—I hope they all go to heaven, so there is a big rodeo in the sky, but with mechanical bulls. Let's be kind to animals once and for all.

Craft—Learn a hobby and you won't be bored.

Cranky—Don't pay any attention to cranky people, because then they will realize their crankiness is not doing them any good.

Crawl—Mental illness does this to you. Other people may see you walking, but when you are afflicted with mental illness, you are crawling. I should know—I crawled down that road and survived.

Cream—You may not be the cream of the crop. Who cares so long as you keep up with the crop?

Credit card—You can buy with it, but you can't pay for your purchase later with it.

Crime—Stop it in its tracks; develop a neighborhood watch.

Crisis—To overcome a crisis, you need a level head, so practice clear thinking, and you may put it to good use later.

Criticism—Don't criticize unless you can do something better.

Cross—Christ died on one, so don't be afraid of one.

Crow—People who eat enough crow won't brag so much.

Crown—Some people you would like to put crowns on their heads; others you would like to stick the crown someplace else.

Cruel—Don't be cruel, because there is enough pain in the world already.

Crutch—It is all right to use a crutch when you need one in order to walk, but don't use any other kind of crutch to make it through life.

Cub Scout—A wonderful training ground to teach young boys how to do good things for other people.

Cultivate—Develop your mind so you can harvest a good crop of thinking in years to come.

Cup—If your cup runneth over, pour the spillover into the cup of another person who needs it.

Cupid—Don't play cupid if you can't keep your own true love contented.

Cure-all—For the soul, it's confession; for the body, it's saying no when it hurts.

Curfew—Don't give your children hell for missing the curfew; just thank God they're home. There is no such thing as a curfew to parents of missing children.

Curtain call—Just because you're not applauded at work doesn't mean your co-workers don't appreciate you. Maybe there is silent applause going for you every day.

Cushy—Your job may not be cushy, but at least you've earned your keep.

Cut—When you throw junk mail away, be sure you cut out your name and address. That way nobody can get your name and address and use it for whatever purpose they have in mind.

D

Dairy—When you eat a dairy product, remember the work that went into it and maybe you will appreciate and help the family farms.

Dampen—Don't depress anybody, because we need all the lively people to establish a more livable world.

Dance—Everybody can dance; just move your feet in whatever direction you want and you are dancing, no matter what anybody says.

Dare—Dare to be brave and you will.

Dark—Don't be afraid of the dark, because fear doesn't come from darkness; it comes from inside of you and you can control it if you want to.

Dash—Years ago it was dashing through the snow in a one-horse open sleigh; nowadays it's skidding across the road in a lemon of a car.

Date—Every day on the calendar should be a happy one for you, because it is one more day the Lord has made, so rejoice and be glad in it.

Dazzle—Don't be so overpowered by something that you can't tell what is reality and what is fantasy.

Death—When people die, they don't go to their destiny alone. Your love for them goes with them, and they leave behind their love for generations to enjoy forever.

December—The month of Christmas joy. It should be a month-long birthday celebration in honor of Jesus Christ.

Decision—If you are an indecisive person, don't feel bad, because choosing to be indecisive is a decision. You decided not to make up your mind.

Deep—Have a deep love for country, fellow man, nature, and animals, and you will do all right in life.

Deer—I prefer to see deer loose and running in the wild rather than stiff and flopped over a car going fifty-five miles an hour or more down the road.

Defend—Thanks to the millions of soldiers who defended our country in war in order for the rest of us to enjoy freedom in America.

Degrade—It is much better to upgrade than to degrade.

Deliver—Don't tell jokes if you can't tell the punch lines the way they should be told.

Demands—Don't make demands on people that even you can't fulfill.

Demonstrate—Show your willingness to work with other people, because it is only through cooperation that success is achieved.

Dentist—Don't be afraid of the dentist, because if you don't go to one, you may eventually see your teeth floating around in a water-filled glass at night.

Depend—Be someone people can count on, and you will be a more responsible person.

Depression—Don't allow yourself to lie in the gutter too long, because before long you will become part of the gutter.

Depth—It isn't how much love you show for somebody but the quality of love that counts.

Desert—Don't knock the wasteland. After all, there's water in the cactus and there's no lawn to cut.

Dessert—Don't eat too much of this, because instead of coming to the table to eat, you will be the table.

Destroy—It is better to build than to destroy.

Determine—Decide how much effort you want to put into something before you start doing it. If it isn't enough, don't start it, because efforts not spent in a worthwhile manner are efforts better "spent" not at all.

Develop—See to it your children have the proper education, because the proper development of a child's mind means a brighter future for the world.

Devour—Don't eat up everything in sight, because your sight may be deceiving you and you may become a devourer of unhealthy substances.

Diabetics—They have a hard road to go, because we all like sweets. I wish them luck.

Dial—Make sure you dial the right number when you use the telephone, because it may be hard for the other party to get to the phone.

Diamonds—The diamonds people wear are not as great as the diamond you can have within: Jesus Christ.

Dictionary—Anybody can write a book. A book is just the dictionary with the words all mixed up and some repeated.

Diet—In America, a lot of people diet to be thin. If we lived in Africa, we wouldn't have to worry about that.

Difficulty—When you overcome a difficult task, the joy is more than overcoming a lesser one.

Dime—It was nice years ago when you could buy a cup of coffee for a dime. Now all you can get for a dime is an eyedropperful of coffee.

Dining room—You don't need a dining room in which to eat food. Just be thankful you have something to eat.

Direction—Know the direction of your life. Then when you change your mind about something you will know the way home again.

Disarm—Wouldn't it be nice if all countries would disarm? It's frightening to think the fate of millions is in the hands a few. Believe in God and it will be in his hands alone.

Discipline—It's all right to be strict, but don't discipline your children out of the home and into the street.

Discount—Just remember something on discount may be on last count—in other words, on its way out.

Disease—Let's work together to wipe it all out.

Dishes—So what if you don't have china to eat off? Just be thankful you have something to eat.

Dishwasher—Don't feel bad if you don't have a dishwasher and have to wash dishes by hand. Some people with arthritis wish they could wash dishes.

Dismiss—Don't send away anything that can't be replaced.

Distance—Shorten the distance between the people you love by sending a card or telephoning them.

Disturb—Don't bother anybody unless some goodwill comes out of it.

Ditch—Don't knock people who dig ditches. After all, some of them are building the future homes for many of us.

Divorce—Don't despair. Begin again.

Do—Try to do what is right for you, and I am sure it will be right for everybody else, too.

Dock—If your ship hasn't come in yet, maybe you are looking for the wrong kind of ship. Maybe you should be looking for a canoe instead of a yacht.

Doctor—A good one is worth a million dollars and then some. I have a good one.

Dogcatchers—Don't blame the dogcatchers for anything. After all, in many cases they are just rounding up strays people let run loose.

Doghouse—Stick yourself in a real doghouse outside during the wintertime, and you will see how some animals have to live.

Dolphin—They are beautiful animals to see perform.

Domestic—If you can do your own work, do it. The time comes soon enough when somebody else has to do your work.

Dominate—Don't dominate anybody. Everybody has the right to be themselves.

Doors—Keep your doors locked at all times. People should be welcome at your house, but on your terms, not theirs.

Dope—It is bad enough to have to take medicine when you are sick. That some people take drugs to get a kick out of it doesn't make sense.

Double-cross—Don't double-cross anybody unless making promises doesn't mean anything to you. Shame on you if it doesn't.

Doubt—Don't doubt anything until you see the proof of the pudding.

Dough—I like to eat the dough right out of the bowl before anything is made out of it.

Dove—A white dove will always be the symbol of peace to me.

Down—The next step is up.

Draft—Let people go into service on their own, and they will march to their own tune, not somebody else's.

Drain—If something is draining you, unplug it with the strength you have within.

Drama—The real drama is in the world, not on a stage or screen.

Draw—Anybody can draw. If you know what the picture is of, who cares if nobody else does?

Drawbridge—If the drawbridge of your life is raised, learn to pole-vault.

Drawers—Don't put your hands in anybody's drawers unless you are married to the owner of the drawers.

Dread—If you dread doing something that has to be done, the sooner you do it, the better off you'll be.

Dream—Dreams are free, so the sky is the limit.

Drift—It's okay to drift from shore, but don't stay away so long that you don't recognize it when you return.

Drop—A drop in the bucket is better than nothing at all.

Drum—It is okay to beat your own drum, but don't beat it so hard even your own ears can't stand it.

Duck soup—It may be duck soup today. But be prepared, for tomorrow may be like nailing Jell-O to a wall.

Due—Pay what you owe anybody and go home with a clear conscience.

Dull—If something is dull, be like a rainbow and brighten it up.

Dump—Don't dump your troubles on anybody else, because when you handle your own troubles, you grow as a person.

Dust—When the weeds start growing on top of the refrigerator, it's time to dust.

Duty—It's your duty to conduct yourself in a way so your parents will be proud to call you their own.

Dwarf—Most of them are giants in the way they conduct themselves in the world. They have turned their scars into stars.

Dying—Dying is nothing to be scared of, because it is a part of life and indicates a new direction.

Dynamic—Use all the energy you have to make it a better world for everyone and everything.

E

Eager—Be eager to go in the morning, and you won't be stopped at any potential pitfalls.

Eagle—Be like an eagle and soar in the heights, and you won't miss the pleasure of reaching the top.

Ear—Hear what you want to, but don't blame anybody else but yourself for what you miss.

Early—The early bird catches the worm, but not too early, because the bird needs strength to catch the worm.

Earth—Take care of it so some space is left for the next generation.

Ease—Ease the pain of others through your willingness to accept some of it yourself.

Easter—You can rise from the dead, and with a soul filled with grace, you can become part of eternal life.

Easy—Make life easier for somebody, and the reward for you will be the joy you see on his face.

Eat—Eat all you want, but don't blame anybody but yourself when you have to buy clothes from Omar the Tentmaker.

Echo—May all the echoes in your life repeat what you want to hear.

Economy—Let's hope for the day when everybody has the same standard of living.

Ecstatic—Show great delight when something good happens to someone else. We are all trying to make it through the night.

Edge—The advantage can be yours if you work hard and keep a cool head.

Edit—If you find yourself working too hard, edit out some work time and take the time you need for some pleasure.

Education—You need it, so learn it and use it every day of your life.

Efficient—Be effective when you are assigned something, and you will see people trusting you. An efficient person can handle responsibility.

Effort—Use your energy wisely, because your achievement will show how wisely you used it.

Egg—Get more baskets and spread your eggs around.

Elapse—Don't let time pass without taking notice, because each moment is precious.

Elastic—Be flexible and show your courage for change.

Electoral College—I think elections should be won by the popular vote, not the electoral college. After all, we are all citizens of the United States, not just the people who live in the states with the most electoral votes.

Electricity—If your lights go out, light a candle and remember the warmth. Let darkness be a remembrance of warmth, not coldness.

Elements—If you use the right elements daily, your progress in life will be daily, too.

Elephants—Elephants may look clumsy and overweight, but look at the joy they have brought to millions.

Elevators—I don't like elevators, but I suppose we need them to keep up with the skyscrapers. To me, they are like closets on the move.

Eliminate—I hope when you delete something, you have good recall in case you need it again later on.

Elite—Don't worry if you aren't part of an elite group, because you know what your best is. Your best may be better than the elite's best.

Embargo—Don't let anybody or anything prohibit your goal of being you to your complete self. Nobody can be you better than you can.

Embark—Every day is a journey you take. Offer up everything you do for the glory of God, and he will smooth out your road for a safe journey.

Embassy—God bless those who serve overseas, because they are serving us so we can have freedom in America.

Emergency—Don't freak out when there is an unforeseen situation that requires immediate action. Stay cool, calm, and collected, and you will see the results you want.

Emigration—I wish everybody's homeland was home to them and not a reign of terror, causing people to flee from their homelands.

Emotions—They keep you going. Just keep them on an even keel, and you will do all right.

Empire State Building—Some people come at you like the Empire State Building, but don't let that bother you. Look what David did to Goliath.

Empty—Don't live a life without meaning. Fill your life with activities that will put feeling into your life. God helps those who help themselves.

Enchantment—Don't be so charmed by something that you can't tell the difference between reality and fiction.

Encouragement—Give courage to those who need it in order to survive.

Encyclopedia—Read it and learn about new avenues of life.

Endorsement—Give your support to ideas that mean betterment for all.

Endurance—If you have a high endurance rate, help those that don't.

Enhance—Improve the surroundings around you for a more beautiful world.

Enjoy—Enjoy life, for laughing is the key to breaking up a sad world.

Enlightener—Be one and help delete ignorance from life.

Enough—Make your goal in life enough food for everybody.

Entertainer—Anybody can be an entertainer. If you make people laugh, you are one.

Enthusiasm—Don't hide it if you want to inspire, because an eager mind is the road for people to follow.

Entrance—May the doorway to your house be the peace the people who enter are looking for.

Entrust—Entrust your love to people who appreciate it and will care for it.

Envelope—Before you seal an envelope, make sure you are satisfied with the contents, because once an envelope is sealed and on its way, you are no longer in control of it.

Envy—Don't desire anybody else's advantages, because if you take your own qualities into account and build on them, you should do all right.

Equality—I think in South Africa they should read the Bible, because it says everybody is born equal. There are no exceptions to the rule.

Erect—Build up in your mind a foundation for positive thinking, and do wonders for the world.

Eskimos—They teach how to live with just the bare necessities.

Essential—Knowing who you are, where are you now, and where you want to go is a must.

Establish—Pattern your life so people can look up to you as an example to be followed.

Estimate—Find out how much practice it takes for you to live up to your highest potenial.

Eternity—Be good and you can have this.

Ethics—Everybody should be treated ethically.

Eucharist—Receive it daily. It is only through the receiving of the body of Christ that we can become the body of ourselves.

Euthanasia—Before you end somebody's life, think of whose pain you are considering. Is it the suffering your loved one is going through, or is it the pain you are going through from watching him suffer? God never gives anybody more pain than he can handle. God loves those who are suffering and will take care of them.

Even—We all start out this way, but along the way things aren't distributed the way they should be. So hang onto your hats as you march on.

Evil—Avoid this as much as possible. Why fight temptation when you don't have to?

Excel—Find what you are good at, and give it all you can.

Exchange—Get in the habit of exchanging friendly greetings with people, and you will be the cheerer-upper they need.

Excuses—Don't make excuses for mistakes you know you made. It is a waste of time. Admit your mistake and go on from there.

Executive—Don't feel bad if you are not an executive, with your own office. Some executives can play marbles at noontime and don't have to go to a store to buy them.

Exist—With mental illness you just exist. Overcome it and live again.

Experience—The only experience gained is from presence on-the-job. Never say to a person that he doesn't have any experience. How can he get any if you don't hire him?

Expert—It isn't how much you know that makes an expert. It's how you apply what you know that counts.

Express—Express yourself when it will make a difference in your life for the betterment of others.

Explain—Don't try to explain your existence. God put you here for a purpose.

Explore—Explore your mind; you might find some area unexplored before.

Extend—Stretch your hand out to a person in need.

Eye—Take care of your eyes, for they are the sight of your future.

Fact—The facts of life should be explained to a child when he asks about it. We gain nothing from ignorance. Everything is gained from knowledge.

F

Fail—You only fail when you don't go on after making a mistake.

Fair—Be fair in your dealings, and you will have a clear conscience.

Faith—Everybody that drives a car has faith. They believe when they put on the brakes, the car will stop.

Fall—It was meant for the leaves to fall, not you.

Falsify—Don't falsify anybody's hopes, because when you do a candle that was lighting the darkness is out.

Family—In our family, we didn't say, "I love you" too much, because we knew the love was there. We didn't need any assurances of its presence.

Fame—Don't be jealous of well-known people. Everything comes out in the wash. In a hundred years, they will be stiffer than all get out.

Fancy—Fancy doesn't count when it comes to real value. You don't have to put up a front for anything worthwhile.

Far—Shorten the distance between you and a loved one. Use the telephone.

Farmer—A person who grows food for thought. Without food, you can't think, because you wouldn't have any strength, so appreciate the farmers of the world.

Fashion plate—A fashion plate is okay as long as you know where the fashion ends and the person begins.

Fear—If you are afraid of something, ask yourself why and then try to overcome it.

Feeling—Something that comes with the turf of being a human being.

Fence—Make sure the fence you put up is on your property, not in your mind.

Field—It is all right to play the field, but make sure you remember to cultivate once in a while.

Fighting—Peace is so much better.

File clerk—This job is crucial, because important paperwork must be put in the right place.

Final—Nothing is final until the fat lady sings, and if you see her start to sing, tell her not to come back until she goes on a diet.

Find—Find your heart and pass out the love in it.

Fine—If you are fine, quit your complaining.

Finger—Don't point your finger at anybody. Your fingers were meant for doing, not pointing.

Finish—Don't start anything you can't finish, because the finish line was meant to cross, not avoid.

Fire—Fight fire by saying a Rosary, saying the Stations of the Cross, or reading the Bible.

Fire fighters—They risk their lives every day, so show kindness and gratitude to them every day.

Firmness—Be firm, but don't let it rule out gentleness if your firmness proves to be too much.

First—It doesn't matter where you place, just so you give it your best.

Flag—Be proud of the flag; the ones who fought for it were proud of it.

Flock—Be part of the flock, for without you, they are not as strong as they could be.

Flower—Send some to somebody who needs a bouquet of love to make it through the night.

Focus—Focus your eyes on things that will enlighten your world, not darken it.

Fog—If the fog level in your head is too high, remember to turn the headlights on.

Follow—Follow your dreams and if you come to a dead end, build your own overpass and keep going.

Food—Don't deny people the power to think. The lack of food does this. Help to see that everybody has the power to think.

Fool—They say a fool is born every day, but remember, it takes two fools to create a fool.

Foot—Take care of your feet; look at the weight they have to carry.

Force—Don't use force unless in self-defense or when somebody else is in trouble.

Forget—If you are having a hard time remembering things, see a doctor, because the key to making it through the night is remembering the good times.

Forgive—If Our Father in Heaven can forgive you when you sin, you too can forgive those who trespass against you.

Forty—People say life begins at forty. The only thing I wish is I would have known at twenty the things I know now.

Forward—March on towards your ideas and place in the sun.

Foundation—Build a strong foundation and if you ever fall in the gutter, you will have the strength to pull yourself out.

Frame—Be in the right frame of mind every day, and you can accomplish anything.

Freak—If you think somebody is a freak, maybe you should take a hard look at yourself in a mirror.

Freedom—America. What else can I say?

Friend—Be a friend to somebody that doesn't have one.

Frown—Don't frown when a smile would do you and everybody else you meet so much more good.

Frustration—This only causes a waste of time in getting something accomplished.

Fuel—If people would put as much effort into their work as they do when it comes to quitting time, think of what could be accomplished. The products of America would be so good there wouldn't be any competition from foreign markets. "Made in the U.S.A." would be just as common a phrase as "Born in the U.S.A."

Full—Remember to keep your gas tank full, especially at night and in the wintertime.

Funeral home—Have you ever walked into a funeral home and thought a party was going on? Why does it take a person's departing before some people arrive on the scene?

Furnish—Be the provider you were meant to be, and you will see results that will provide you with a smile.

Fury—Don't be like the fury of a storm when the calmness of the sea will accomplish just as much.

Future—Your future depends on what you do today.

G

Gain—Earn your place in the sun; then when the sun's rays shine on you, you know the warmth was meant for you.

Gallery—So what if your paintings aren't in a gallery? You paint to enjoy them, not to impress others.

Gambling—Excess gambling means the loss of the chance to live right.

Game—A game is meant for fun and enjoyment, not for blood, sweat, and tears.

Gangplank—If you can swim, going off the gangplank isn't so bad.

Garden—May the seeds of life you plant produce the accomplishments of tomorrow you desire.

Gather—Let us all gather together and send a message of peace to the rest of the world.

Generation—Let's hope for generation after generation that peace will reign supreme all over the world.

Gentlemen—Marry one and you will see the difference between gentlemen and not so gentle men.

Give—Give until it hurts; then you will be satisfied you did your part in making the world a better place for all.

Glad—Be glad if you can get out of bed in the morning and be the person God wants you to be.

Glee club—Join a glee club if you want to sing. The joy you bring others is worth all the practice time. I wanted to sing in the glee club in high school, but some older kids kept picking on me, so I quit. I wasn't very brave when I was young. What I should have done was turn around and punch them in the nose. When you want to do something, never give in to the stupidity of others.

Glitter—All that glitters isn't gold, but enjoy the sparkle anyway.

Glory—Glory to God always.

Glutton—Don't eat more than you can handle.

God—Father or mother of us all. Let God be the gender you desire.

Going—Go where your heart desires.

Good—Be good and see the joy your goodness brings to others.

Good looks—Everyone is good-looking in their own way.

Good-bye—Never think of this as farewell, because you have to meet someone before you can say good-bye. Remember the meeting, not the parting.

Goose—Don't goose anybody or the goose you cook may be your own.

Gossip—Don't feel bad if people gossip about you, because if they are talking about you, they aren't talking about anyone else.

Grace—Give thanks for the blessings provided to you.

Graduate—If you didn't have an opportunity to go to college, high school, or even grade school, don't feel bad. Every day you live you advance as a human being.

Grandparents—Grandparents like to brag about their grandchildren but don't feel bad if you don't have any. It isn't the number of grandchildren you have that counts; it's the love you share with children that don't have anybody else to love.

Greatest—I once thought the greatest thing you could be in life was the president, a movie star, or a king or queen, but that isn't true. The greatest thing you can be in life is yourself to the best of your ability. That is all the master desires.

Greedy—Be greedy, but for the needy.

Greenhorn—Give a greenhorn a break. He has to start somewhere.

Grief—Overcome your grief with prayers from the heart.

Ground—With your feet flat on the ground and a firm grip on yourself, grind out your problems and your troubles will go away.

Group—A unit of people, with each one capable of thinking as a single unit.

Grow—Every day we grow as people.

Guard—Put on your defense against sin, and keep the scoreboard saying zero on the bad side.

Guide—Be the guide dog to those who have lost sight of their prospects.

Guitar—Make someone happy by playing a song for them if you can.

Gum—If you can't chew gum and walk at the same time, so what?

Gun—Don't use one unless in self-defense.

Gymnasium—If you can't exercise in your home, go to a gym and get the exercise you need, or maybe you have a job where you get enough exercise.

H

Habit—Develop good habits and you will find yourself living a better life.

Hail—Hail, hail, the gang's all here, and when they come, greet them with open arms. Have a party and serve nonalcoholic beverages. Be sure to keep the noise down so you don't disturb the neighbors.

Halt—Put a stop to things that corrupt the minds of children.

Hand—Shake hands with a friend and say, "Peace be with you," and tell him to pass it on.

Handicap—A person may be bodily handicapped, but nothing can handicap your spirit.

Handle—If you keep your handle on, you won't fly off the handle.

Handsome—It's all right to be good-looking, but don't let your good looks change how you treat other people. Beauty built from within doesn't change with age like beauty on the outside does.

Harmony—If everybody worked together, war would become obsolete.

Haste—Don't make haste if it means leaving a mess a mile long.

Haunt—Don't allow memories to haunt you. What is done is done.

Headache—Don't fake one because to people who get them all the time, headaches are not so funny.

Headline—Your daily life may not make the headlines, but you are a headliner in God's world.

Heart—Sometimes it takes trying from the bottom of your heart to show the love of which you are capable.

Heaven—A place where dreams are made.

Heavy—Don't be too heavy, because people will see your fatness before they see you.

Heel—Some people are heels, so don't let them become your shoes.

Height—It doesn't matter how tall you are. Your ideas may make up for what you lack in height.

Hemorrhoids—Some people are like hemorrhoids.

Hercules—If you can't look like Hercules, then think like Hercules. The strength of the mind can move mountains.

Heredity—Never blame your mistakes on heredity. You are an individual, so be responsible for you.

Hero—Everybody is a hero. Getting up every morning and facing the world takes courage beyond compare.

Hesitate—Don't take too long to decide something, because opportunity might pass you by.

Hide—Never hide from anything unless you're playing hide and go seek.

High—Get high on the playing field, not in the driving lanes.

Hinder—Never hinder anyone unless hindrance is the key in preventing a mistake.

History—In the history books all the presidents of the United States are listed, but everybody, past, present, and future, is part of history. You don't have to be listed in a history book to know you have made a contribution to society.

Hit—Hit only in self-defense.

Hobby—Have one and you will make "Bore time" into "Joy time."

Hold fast—Hold fast to the principles that have brought you this far.

Hole—Sometimes when you are in a hole, you have to dig deeper before you can get out.

Holiness—Mother Theresa is an example of this. Her goodness will reign forever.

Hollywood—Where people get paid for doing things that in real life they would get arrested for.

Holocaust—The memory and spirit of those lost in the Holocaust will go on forever.

Homemaker—A beautiful career and don't let anybody tell you otherwise.

Honesty—Honesty pays off when the truth comes out.

Honeymoon—The honeymoon is over when your lovemaking sessions are counted by the years instead of days.

Hooray—Hooray for Hollywood when they make a clean, family picture.

Hope—Live today because of the hope of tomorrow.

Horse—A horse may wear blinders, but don't let the blinders in life keep you from seeing anything.

Hospital—A good place to be if you are sick.

Hostage—How come when terrorists hijack a plane, they let everybody go except the men? Some of the women could handle the terrorists just as well as the men. Men aren't emotionally strong all the time, and women aren't emotionally weak all the time.

House—A house is not a home until you have a foundation of love.

How—Don't ask how; just do it.

Hug—Hug someone special when they need reassurance of your love for them.

Human brain—The computer is trying to replace this, but it will never make the grade, because something God-made excels something man-made every time.

Humble—Eat some humble pie, but leave some for someone else, because you're not alone.

Humor—Add some cheer to your life, and make others laugh.

Hurdle—Learn to jump and you will learn how to jump any hurdle in your life.

Hurt—Don't do anything to anybody that you wouldn't want done to yourself.

Hyena—If you hear someone laughing like a hyena, find out why and maybe you can spread the laughter.

I

Ideas—Don't let your ideas go to waste. Act on them and you will see the fruits of your labor.

Idleness—Idle time is the devil's workshop. I sometimes think the way the world is sometimes, his workshop must be overflowing.

Ignition—May the ignition of your career goals be fired up and ready to go at all times.

Illness—If you are sick and aren't getting better, see your doctor and then put your faith in the Doctor of Us All.

Illustrate—Show an example for others to follow as you journey through life.

Imitation—Don't be an imitation of yourself. People want to see the real thing.

Immediate—If the world would try to be one big immediate family, we would not have to worry about war.

Immunization—Protect yourself against anything that would want to see you succumb to the temptations of evil. A warehouse of grace built up in your soul is the greatest immunization system of all.

Impede—Obstruct Satan as he tries to spread his evil work on the earth.

Importance—I don't care how important a person is or thinks he is. When he dies the world will keep on going. Look at the president of the United States—the world doesn't stop for him or her.

Impose—Don't place a burden on anybody. Take care of your own and if you have strength left over, help somebody else.

Impossible—Anything is possible if you set your mind to it.

Impression—Make a good imprint on somebody's mind, and you will be a source of delight for them when they see you.

Improper—Always show good taste and your way of doing things will be accepted by those that could make a difference in your life.

Improve—Make better what you can; accept what you can't.

Impulse—Make sure the force you exert pushes you in the right direction.

In crowd—Don't feel bad if you don't belong to the in crowd. Some of the people who belong to the in crowd would have to go to a dark room with a flashlight to find their brains.

Incest—Help is needed for both the victim and the aggressor. Report it either if you see it or if it is happening to you. Silence is not golden when it comes to incest.

Income Tax—Money paid so the government can pay for some more chauffeur-driven limousines for the big shots in government.

Incurable—Anything can be cured as long as the mind hangs on to hope.

Independent—Be this way, but be willing to accept help when you need it.

India—I wish the people in India and Africa had enough to eat.

Indian Giver—The government is this. It prints the money we earn at our jobs; then it takes it away in taxes.

Indulge—Eat all the sweets you want, but it is time to stop when you have more rolls than your local bakery.

Inferiority Complex—Get help if this makes you feel like a fish without water.

Inform—Keep your mind informed of the events going on around you.

Inherit—What you earned is more important than what you waited for.

Injustice—Try to correct the unfairness in the world. Where there is injury, be the healing bandage needed for the wound.

Innocent—Protect the innocent, for they are the children of tomorrow.

Insignificant—People who bother you.

Inspiration—People who don't bother you.

Instinct—Use your instinct to use the right values in life as you wage war against the struggles in your life.

Institution—Visit one and when you come out, count your blessings.

Instruction—Teach those who need to know the right directions to the right goal in their lives.

Instrument—Be an instrument of peace, so you are doing your part for all of God's children to live in peace.

Insurance—This costs too much and when you try to collect you can't bank on anything.

Insure—Thanks go to veterans who insured us the right to live in freedom in America.

Intelligence—We are all born with it; we just have to learn how to develop it.

Intent—Don't be afraid to change your mind if your intentions don't serve the purpose you had in mind.

Interest—Let your interests be your guide in obtaining what is best for you.

Interference—Run interference when you think it will do somebody some good.

Introduction—Don't be afraid to say who you are, because nobody can be you better than you can.

Investment—Make strong investments, because they are what you live on when the time comes.

Involve—Involve yourself with projects that will make the whole world better.

Ironing board—Don't let it bother you if you are flat-chested. Some women who have had their breasts removed because of cancer are living normal and productive lives.

Itinerary—May your plan for life include thanking your God for the blessings bestowed on you.

J

Jack—Jack up your life every day by putting forth the best effort you can.

Jam—If your life becomes jammed, reach out your hand for the Lord to give you a hand.

Janitors—They make the floors we take for granted sparkle, those floors we never notice until they are dirty. Why not thank the janitor when floors are clean instead of bitching when they are dirty.

Jaywalk—Don't jaywalk, because it it easy to get hit by a car.

Jealous—Jealousy doesn't serve any purpose except to demean you as a human being.

Jerks—Jerks are developed, not born, so don't let this development overtake you.

Jet Set—If you feel comfortable in the caboose why worry about the jets flying overhead? It doesn't matter what your style is; just enjoy it. You are the one living with it.

Jewel—Be the jewel God meant you to be.

Jockey—I think the jockeys should let the horses ride once in a while. Fair is fair.

Judges—I wish judges wouldn't throw cases out on technicalities.

Judgment Day—On this day, God is going to give out Oscars even Hollywood can't match. They will be for the people who care for other people more than themselves.

Junk—Remember, you are good; God doesn't make any junk.

Justice of the Peace—If you can't wait to get married, I suppose a justice of the peace will do in a pinch. But later have the kind of ceremony your heart desires.

K

Keep—Keep trying to do your best, and you will make out okay.

Key—Keep your heart unlocked so you don't need a key. Love should be free and flowing, not locked up and still.

Kindness—Show it and the happiness you bring will be reward enough.

King—There is only one and he is the Father of Us All.

Knife—This was meant for cutting up food, not people.

Knight—If you ever see a knight on a white horse, you will know fairy tales really do come true.

Knock—Check out the window before you answer a knock at the door.

Knockdown—Don't let a knockdown shortchange you on your way to success in life.

Knot—Tie a good one around hatred, and never let it go.

Know—Know you are wanted, even though people don't show it.

L

Labor—Make everything a labor of love, and the results will be music to your ears.

Lack—If you lack something, work at it until it is the level you want.

Lady—A woman who knows inside she is polite, refined, and well mannered, but doesn't have to put on a big front to prove it.

Land—Wars are fought over land, which is lifeless and can't show love. In wars, people are killed in wars, who were alive and could show love. This is crazy, purely crazy.

Lantern—May the lantern you light, provide the light for some wayward soul.

Last—There's nothing wrong with last that first won't cure, because in the Bible it says the last shall be first.

Late—You may be late, but at least you show up.

Lawyer—They charge a lot. A person never knows how much is for air and how much is for quality.

Leaders—If it wasn't for the followers, there wouldn't be anybody to lead.

Leaves—They are beautiful in the fall. Why don't we pay attention to them until they change colors? Why do we need change before we notice something? Why can't we accept things for what they are?

Learn—Every day you learn something new, and your growth as a human being keeps on going.

Leave—Don't leave anybody or anything behind that you know can't take care of themselves.

Leg—The secret to life is to keep the legs moving.

Legends—In God's eyes we are all legends.

Lemon—If the American car manufacturers would make decent cars, the American people wouldn't be forced to buy foreign ones.

Level-headed—No matter what kind of a head you have, just be thankful you have the power to think with it.

License—Be sure you have a license for anything that requires one.

Life—Don't take life too seriously. You're not going to get out of it alive.

Light—It is better to turn on a light than to shut one off.

Like—It doesn't matter who likes you or not, just so you have enough pride to make it through the night.

Limit—There is a limit to everything, but don't let it stop you from making the progress you are working for in life.

Line—Hold the line and walk the line, but don't skip the line.

Link—Make sure all your links are strong. Your hookup to life depends on them.

Lip—Take care of your lips. You kiss with them and talk with them. Most important of all you keep your mouth shut with your lips.

Little—Don't judge people by their size. A lot of little people are shaping the world today.

Lively—Be lively. It is better than being deadly.

Load—Fill your head with knowledge, and save this knowledge for a rainy day.

Loan—Don't borrow too much. The paying back can be killing if you don't have the money.

Local—The action starts at the local level before it spreads to the national level, so don't downplay the local touch.

Logic—Use it and enjoy it.

Long-distance—Beautiful memories can shorten the distance between you and your loved ones.

Look—Watch out for the booby traps in life.

Loons—I like loons. The sound they make is worth more than the millions of words spoken every day.

Lose—You never lose something that you don't gain something from it.

Lounge—Why do some companies make the restrooms for women fancier than those for men? Don't they realize men like to sit in chairs and lie down on couches, too?

Lottery—How come people don't pay any attention to you until you win a lottery?

Low—It's all right to lay low sometimes, but don't let it become a habit.

Luck—Don't depend on luck when hard work will insure the results you want.

Lure—Don't be lured unless you know what awaits you.

Lust—It's all right to lust for something. But don't let this lust be fulfilled if you know it's wrong.

M

Machine—Work hard, but don't become like a machine. Machines can't love and you can and need to take time out for your feelings once in a while.

Mad money—Money put aside so you can afford to act crazy once in a while.

Magnetism—Let your mind be like a magnet, picking up and storing what is needed for you to be the person you want to be.

Mail—Use the mail service. I would hate to see it go down the tube. I look forward to the mail every day. It either makes or breaks my day.

Make—Bake a cake and bring it to a person you know it will bring cheer to.

Malice—Don't create any more evil in the world than there is already.

Malignant—If you have a growth that is malignant, keep up your spirits and know you are not alone. You are part of the in crowd, the in crowd of courageous people.

Maneuver—Maneuver your way to the top, then help those down below make it to the top, too.

Mantle—May your mantle reflect what is good about life, not what is bad.

Manuscript—May the manuscript of your life read like a Bible.

Marathon—Whether you are in a marathon or marching to your own tune, just keep doing it, for exercise is the best policy.

Margin—Be sure when you provide for the needy, it is by a wide margin.

Marines—God bless them, because they are what being brave is all about.

Mark—Make sure the mark you leave betters the quality of life for all and isn't easily erased.

Market—If the market falls, don't feel bad if you have your health. If you are healthy, you have the best blue chip stock in the world.

Mass—Go to mass; it is good for the soul.

Marriage—When a couple want to spend their lives together, with their love for each other being their guide as they journey through life together.

Marshalls—I hope they have the strength to do their job corrrectly.

Mask—Wear one at Halloween, but don't hide behind one the rest of your life.

May—A beautiful month to gather flowers in.

Mean—Don't be mean when kindness would be so much better.

Measure—Don't measure people by their weaknesses. Strengths are better to judge people by.

Medal—Not every good deed gets a medal. Some people go through life doing good for others without getting recognized for it, for their recognition is not of this world but the next.

Medicine—Take your medicine when you are sick, because years of hard work went into learning how to mix the right prescription for you and everbody else.

Member—Be a member of good standing of the human race.

Mend—You can mend a broken heart, but what can you do for a broken mind?

Microscope—Don't be the kind of person who has to examine everything under a microscope before he accepts something as fact.

Mile—Some people suffer such hardship in life that you'd be lucky if you were able to walk a block in their shoes.

Millionaire—You don't have to be a millionaire to enjoy the best things in life, like the sun, stars, et cetera.

Millions—The term "millions" is used for describing how many people watch an event or a star on television. But remember, every one of those people is a somebody.

Mine fields—Don't let the mine fields of life distract you from your goals in life.

Minimum delinquency age—I think this should be lowered if it means children going on trial for murdering other children. If they know right from wrong, they know murder when they commit it.

Misery—Learn to partake in the misery of others, and you will better understand their fate.

Mistress—Why divide your love when devoting all your love to your wife would be more useful for your marriage?

Model—Just because you aren't on a magazine cover doesn't mean you're not a model. Magazine covers are tomorrow's garbage. You are today's news, starring as yourself.

Mold—God made you from a mold that wasn't repeated, because he wanted you to be you. Nobody can be you better than you can.

Money—Some see green. Others see the love for fellowman that money can't buy.

Monk—God bless them, because they pray for us so we can enjoy the world they gave up.

Monopoly—Own all the commodities you want; you still can't take it with you.

Mood—Remember when you're feeling blue, it will pass, because as time passes, so will your mood.

Mop—Don't let your hair look so bad that people will want to tip you upside down and use you as a mop.

Moral—Do what is morally right in life, and you will do all right.

Morning—Bring cheer to people at the beginning of the day and at night, you will be satisfied you did your best.

Mouth—It was meant for talking, but not nonstop.

Murder—Never take a life unless somebody is trying to take yours.

Music—Practice it and someday you will provide the music people will want to hear.

Myrtle—My mother's name is Myrtle. She should have been a nurse, because she is always caring for other people. She never thinks of herself. There would be no troubles in the world if all people were like her.

N

Nag—Don't nag anybody, because life is hard enough.

Name—No matter what your name is, be the person you want to be.

Natural—Be natural, because you never can tell who is watching.

Near—Appreciate your loved ones when they are near, because when they are far away, you know the difference.

Nervous—Get help if your nerves interfere with your life.

Nest—A nest was meant to leave, but don't forget how it was when you are gone.

Nice—Be nice, because a cheerful world is better than a crabby one.

Noise—A party is all right, but show some concern for your neighbors and cut down on the noise.

Noon—So what if you have to brown-bag it? At least you have something to put in the bag; some people have nothing at all.

Normal—Everybody is normal in their own way.

Northern Ireland—The people fighting in Northern Ireland are supposed to be Catholics and Protestants, but they are not. Catholics and Protestants who practice their faith don't act this way.

Nothing—Everybody and everything is something.

Nurse—They can make a difference in your recovery from illness. Remember to thank them before you leave the hospital.

O

Oath—Don't get in the habit of making promises you can't keep.

Obscene phone calls—Don't mess around with them. Tell the police and telephone company, because you never can tell who is waiting at the other end.

Obstacle—A obstacle can be removed if you make up your mind something isn't going to bother you.

Odd—There is beauty in difference. There is nothing odd about it.

Office—Just because you don't have an office doesn't mean your job isn't important. It is a good thing some people are in their own offices, where you can't see them.

Orchestra—Your life should be like an orchestra. During a performance, when a orchestra makes a mistake, they don't quit playing and start over; they keep on playing. That's the way you should be.

Oscar—We don't have to worry about war; just pass on the love that is present during the Academy Award show.

Own—Be your own self and you don't have to worry about people getting the wrong impression of you.

P

Pension—Stay with a company long enough, and you will get one of these. Enjoy it, because you earned it.

Peon—There is no such thing as a peon, because everybody is somebody.

Pep pill—Exercise right, eat right, and get enough sleep; then you won't need a pep pill.

Perfect—Try to be perfect, but don't expect to achieve it, because nobody is perfect except God.

Person—We can each only be one person, which is sad, because maybe you're like me and want to be the whole world.

Pessimism—Think positive and you won't have any trouble with this.

Pheasant—Provide some feed for pheasants in the wintertime, because they provide some of the beauty in nature.

Photography—Be the photographer the world is waiting for.

Physical—Life can be the physical pits sometimes.

Pies—Pies are good, but don't eat too much of them, because it is better to have more of them than you.

Pig—I like pigs, especially little ones.

Pillar—Be the pillar some people need for strength.

Pioneers—They opened up the way of living you have today.

Pipeline—Be a pipeline of peace and pass it on.

Pitcher—It is better to watch a pitcher than to drink one of liquor.

Plain—Nobody is plain. We all possess the beauty of ourselves.

Plan—Develop a plan for your goals in life.

Play—Play fair and make the game enjoyable.

Pledge—Pledge to do your best as you journey through life.

Plug—Keep plugging away every day, and your efforts will pay off.

Plow—Plow through your work every day, and you will enjoy the relaxing time come day's end.

Pocket—Don't pocket anything that doesn't belong to you.

Point—Point to the highest star in the sky, and make it your goal in life to go as high as you can.

Police—They guard the environment so you can enjoy life as you should. Say a prayer for these brave souls tonight.

Politician—Somebody who thinks for himself or herself until election time; then he thinks for everyone else.

Poor—If you have food every day and a roof over your head, you are not poor.

Prepare—Prepare yourself for your older years, and when they come, they will truly be your golden years.

Prostitutes—Don't blame the prostitutes for being on the street. If they didn't have customers, they wouldn't be there.

Psychiatrist—They can give you medicine, but you have to learn how to help yourself.

Q

Quarterback—Don't be a Monday morning quarterback unless you can play on the field with the big boys.

Quit—Don't quit unless you don't want the rewards of success.

Quote—Don't quote anybody too much, because the quote may be out-of-date by the time you say it.

R

Radical—Don't be too radical, because change must walk the true world.

Rape—If this happens to you, find somebody who understands and don't give up until you do.

Reach—Reach out for a hand and help that person through life.

Read—Read all you can, for you may be America's future.

Redouble—Redouble your effort to make it a beautiful world for everybody.

Reflect—Reflect on the pleasant things of life, and your smile will light up the world.

Regard—Send out warm regards to everyone you meet.

Rehearse—Rehearse your behavior as a human being, and you will be a model for the rest of the world to follow.

Release—Release the energy inside you, and the results will be gratifying.

Remember—Remember the good times and be thankful.

Repent—Repent, because if you sinned you should be sorry.

Resource—Save the resources of nature, because once gone, they are gone forever.

Respond—Respond to the needy, because their cause will be your cause.

Retreat—Go on a retreat and review yourself as a human being.

Reverse—When you find yourself going in the opposite direction of that you should be going in, just turn around and go back to where you came from.

Rhythm—Appreciate rhythm, because it can break up the boredom of life.

Right—Be right, but admit it when you are wrong.

Risk—Take a chance and achieve something worthwhile.

Road—If you take the wrong road, make it the right road by making the necessary changes.

Rock of Gibraltar—My brother and his family are like the Rock of Gibraltar, steady and strong when you need them. They help those who need help in this world.

Rolling pin—Good protection against a deadly spouse.

Run-of-the-mill—Nobody is this, because God makes all cream of the crop.

Russia—I wish Russia would mind its own business and let people in other countries run their own lives.

S

Salt—Good for ice and good for the food in your soul.

Sanitary Engineers—They collect your garbage, so be kind to them as they make their morning run. If you have an extra big load, help them carry it to the truck.

Saudi Arabia—I wish we had the oil in America like they do here. I think we should ration gas and car pool now, so we are ready if a shortage ever comes.

Scar—Rename your scar a star.

Seesaw—If this book seems like a seesaw, it is because life is like a seesaw.

Secretary—Don't worry if you can't keep up with the next secretary as far as clothes go. You are there for the quality of your work, not as a fashion plate for the whole world to see.

Sell—Don't sell anything short, because you may end up the shortest of all.

Sex—A beautiful act between a husband and wife.

Shelf—Have the supplies you need to make it through life on your shelves.

Shell—Come out of your shell and come forward.

Shelter—Provide the shelter your family needs to grow up strong and firm in their beliefs.

Ship—Come aboard God's ship. It is beautiful.

Shoplifter—Don't shoplift, because you are just making prices higher for others and yourself. We will never be able to afford to buy anything if shoplifters keep it up.

Shoulder—Share your shoulder with somebody who needs a shoulder to lean on.

Sideline—It's okay to watch from the sidelines, but don't become a permanent fixture on the sidelines.

Signal—May your signal in life be green always.

Simple—Life can be simple; don't complicate it.

Skeletons—Get rid of any skeletons in your closet. You never can tell when somebody else will be cleaning your closet.

Skinny-dip—It's all right to skinny-dip, but be sure when you come out of the water, your skinny-dipping is over.

Slack—Don't slack off when you get ahead. Store your supplies for a rainy day.

Sleepy—Be sure you're not sleepy when driving.

Sloppy—Don't be sloppy when you do something, and you won't have to do it over again.

Smear—Don't smear anything. The cleaning-up process may be difficult.

Smoke—If you like your lungs, don't smoke to excess.

Smorgasbord—Life is like a smorgasbord. You are not going like everything that's "on the table," including people.

Snow—Don't knock it if you've never seen it, and if you've seen it and don't like it, move.

Society—Tries to dictate how everybody should be and live. God made the world for everybody, so what may be "different" in society's eyes may be one individual's cup of tea.

Solid—Be solid where your support is needed and wanted.

Sound—Sound off when somebody is in trouble.

Space—Man goes into space, but I think we should feed the hungry and homeless down here first.

Sparkle—Let the sparkle in your eyes be the lighthouse for others to travel home by.

Sparrow—God's eyes are on the sparrow, so he is watching you, too.

Special—Everybody is special.

Stall—If your car stalls on the highway, wait for the highway patrol. They are God's protectors of the highway. Respect them for the beautiful work they do.

Stereotype—What sex a person is born doesn't mean he or she will always be 100 percent that sex emotionally, so don't make fun of anybody.

Suicide—I hope all suicides find the peace they are seeking.

T

Teacher—They teach America's future. Pay them the wages they deserve.

Touch—Touch only when the other person wants to be touched.

Towns—It makes me mad when people on television say their hometown is such and near a major city that everybody knows. Be proud of your hometown, and don't mention the other city. Your town can stand on its own feet.

Toy—Let your children make their own toys; then they will know the value of doing for themselves at an early age.

Tradition—To hell with tradition. If you want to make a change, go ahead.

Tragedy—Don't let tragic situations stop you. Use your energy and turn them around.

Transform—Transform yourself into the human being you want to be.

Trip—If you want to go on a trip, see all of your home state first. If you don't appreciate what's in your backyard, you'll never appreciate the rest of the world.

Tricks—Don't play tricks unless you are willing to have the same done to you.

Troops—Learn to march like the troops, and you will learn what marching is all about.

Troublemaker—Don't be a troublemaker unless you like life in the slammer.

Truce—All countries should agree to a truce, then watch peace do its thing.

True—Be true to your own true love.

Truly—When you sign a letter "yours truly," mean it with your whole heart.

Trust—Put trust in the one you love.

Try—Try to do your best always.

Tune—Whistle a tune and be happy.

Turn—Make the correct turns and you will follow the correct paths.

Twenty-four-hour store—God is like a store that is open twenty-four hours a day. You can call on him any time of the day or night for help.

Typecasting—Don't typecast anyone. Change is a part of life.

U

Ugly Duckling—Nobody has to be ugly. You are only as ugly as you want to be.

Under—When you are under, can above be far behind?

Uniform—Don't be ashamed to wear a uniform, because the uniform means you are capable of doing the work implied by the uniform.

V

Vandalism—Don't ruin results of the hard work of others.

View—If you think the view from the top is great, you should see it from the bottom.

Vigor—Be vigorous in the morning, and you can conquer your world.

Violin—Anybody who can play it has put years of practice into it.

Voice—Raise your voice when it will make a difference to someone in need.

W

Walk—When you take a walk at night, take a whistle along in case you need it.

Warmth—Be known for the warmth you spread, not the cold you intend sometimes.

Watch—Don't belittle a watch you get for retirement, because you know the hours of effort that you accounted for. No company could ever repay a employee for the dedication put forth.

Water—Save it, because without it we are nothing.

Whale—Save the whales, because their beauty will be missed.

Wheel—A lot of people think they are big wheels, but even a wheel stops when the brakes are put on.

White elephant—Take care of your white elephant, because it may be a precious elephant to someone else.

Wholesome—People who believe in God and sunshine are this.

Why—Don't ask why. Understanding is the key to surviving the "whys" in your life.

Widowhood—This may be a sad time, but don't forget, good moments lived are good memories forever.

Wild goose chase—A wild goose chase isn't so bad. Think of the exercise you get.

Wild oats—Sow your wild oats, but don't forget they're yours come harvest time.

Will—Everybody has a will. Build up a strong one so when problems come your way, you can KO them in their tracks.

Winning—Winning isn't everything, because once you get to the top of the ladder, you go down backwards, so humble yourself for the trip down.

Windows—We are all windows on the world, looking out at what we see. Just remember to keep the glass clean.

Windy—Some people are this. They should inhale more.

Wine—Wine is to be enjoyed, not to pig out on.

Winter—Most people hate it, but when you survive it, you enjoy spring that much more.

Wise—If you are wise, share your wisdom with others for a more productive world.

Wish—Don't wish your life away. Do something positive for somebody, and you won't have time for wishing.

Withdrawal—Don't withdraw into a corner. It is only through life that we are life.

Witness—Be sure the facts you give are true, because it is only through truth that life progresses.

Wolves—If some of your dinner guests eat like wolves, just provide shovels for them instead of silverware.

Wonder—It doesn't hurt to wonder about something. Curiosity doesn't kill the cat. It will make us more aware of where we are going.

Wood—Some people's heads.

Word—If you give a speech, abbreviate your words and make them to the point. People appreciate this more than a windmill running off at the mouth, saying nothing comprehensive.

Work—If you can work, be glad of it, because there are too many people sick in bed who can't work and wish they could.

World—God didn't make an awful world. He made a beautiful one. It is some of the people living in it that make it awful.

Worry—Don't worry about anything. Take one day at a time, and you will make it through life.

Worthy—Make sure you are worthy of the praise given you, because then you will feel so much better accepting it.

Wreck—If you look into a mirror and see this, do something about it, because only you can help yourself.

Wrong—If you are proven to be wrong, accept it and go on from there, vowing to do the right thing whenever possible.

X

X-rated—There must be a demand for X-rated movies, because otherwise they wouldn't be on the market. The day they don't make any money, they will go off the market.

X-ray—Take one of your life, and see if everything is clear. If not, do what you have to do to make it clear.

Y

Yacht—Your boat may not be a yacht, but at least you can sail it.

Yard—Yard work is healthy for you. If are able to do it, do it.

Year—It used to be "Who will care in a hundred years?" Today it is more like "Who will care tomorrow?"

Yell—If you need help, yell, but don't do it if it will endanger your life. Pray silently if you can't yell.

Yellow pages—Use them if your fingers can walk better than your legs.

Yield—Don't be afraid to give in if somebody else is right. If light is produced, what difference does it make who produces it?

You—You are important, because nobody can be you better than you can.

Young—Young at heart is the only age meter that counts.

Yukon—See God's Nature at its best.

Z

Zebra—A zebra has stripes, but that doesn't make it a coward.

Zigzag—If you are doing this while driving, pull over to the side of the road and wait for help to arrive.

Zombie—If you come across one, wake him up and make him aware of the good life.

Zoo—Some places of work are like this.

Zurich—If you can't afford to go there, dream of it. You don't have to have money to dream.